BEAUTIFUL EMPRESS WARRIOR

My Superpower is Love and Kindness

FELISHA SAMS

Beautiful Empress Warrior

My Superpower

is

FELISHA SAMS

Hello, My name is Beautiful!
Love and Kindness is my Superpower.

Here is some of my friends.

WOW, Lets have fun!

I have alot of Friends, you see!

I like to use my Superpower of Love and Kindness.

Do you have a SUPERPOWER?

What is Love? Love is the greatest gift of all.

Love is a good feeling
on the inside of you.

Remember to Love your family and friends.

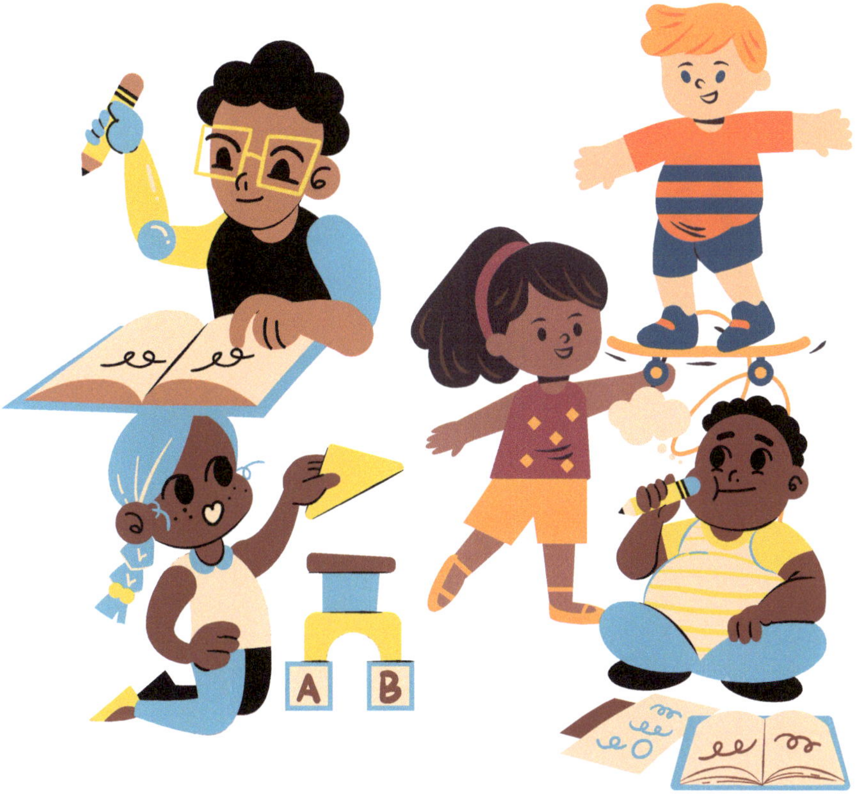

What is Kindness? Being kind to others.

Kindness is being generous and friendly to others.

Kindness is helping others in need and showing sympathy.

This is Mona'e and Lamar.

Mona'e and Lamar was sad about losing their dog Lil Mama. Beautiful to the rescue!

Superpower of Love and Kindness Activate!

Lamar said to Mona'e, "lets think smart and send out love
to Lil Mama".

I send you love and kindness. Mona'e and Lamar think smart and stay happy. I will help you find Lil Mama.

Lil Mama is at the park having fun!

Lamar and Mona'e are happy now. Yes, Lil Mama is back!

Yay, Beautiful helped us find Lil Mama. She used love and kindness.

Lamont, Johnathan, and Kieombra said, Beautiful solves problems and is very genorous.

Desiree,Aaron, Marvin said, Love and kindness is what we needed. Thank you Beautiful!

Oshay and Keisha said, Beautiful has a golden heart. Beautiful used her Superpowers of Love and Kindness to help us all. Yay!

I would like to thank all my friends for believing in me. I'm grateful
I was able to teach you about
love and kindness.

Lamar, Mona'e, and Lamont said, "Wow Beautiful to the rescue"! Beautiful is Love and Kindness.

Hello Friends! I would like to thank you personally for your support. I hope you enjoyed learning about Love and Kindness. What is your superpower? Activate it to help the world. I believe in you.
Beautiful

Beautiful EmpressWarrior Presents
My Superpower is Love and Kindness
FELISHA SAMS

Autograph

Beautiful

www.ingramcontent.com/pod-product-compliance
Lightning Source LLC
Chambersburg PA
CBHW040933110726
48006CB00001B/168